HONOR THY MUSIC®

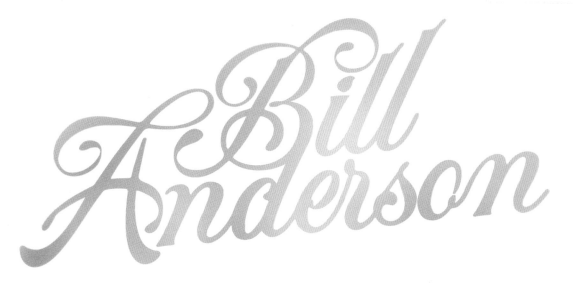

Bill Anderson

AS FAR AS I CAN SEE

COUNTRY MUSIC FOUNDATION PRESS

222 REP. JOHN LEWIS WAY S • NASHVILLE, TENNESSEE 37203

Published 2021. Printed in the United States of America.

978-0-915608-36-2

This publication was created by the staff of the Country Music Hall of Fame® and Museum.

Editor: Paul Kingsbury • Artifact photos by Bob Delevante • Printer: Lithographics, Inc., Nashville, Tennessee

PRINTED IN THE U.S.A. USING SOY-BASED INKS ON ECO-FRIENDLY PAPER

CONTENTS

On the set of *The Bill Anderson Show*, late 1960s
FOREGROUND, FROM LEFT: Jimmy Gateley, Jan Howard, and Bill Anderson
BACKGROUND: Jimmy Lance, Sonny Garrish, and Terry White

Songs highlighted in this book can be found as a Spotify playlist at CountryMusicHallofFame.org/BillAnderson

DEAR MUSEUM FRIEND,

A South Carolina son who came of age in Georgia, Bill Anderson was still in college when he began a journey that would lead him to a place in country music's most hallowed room, the Hall of Fame Rotunda.

He was a young man who found that the ideas that sprang from his fertile mind resonated with people far older than he was. Today, he is an old man (sorry, Bill) who finds the ideas that spring from his fertile mind resonate with people many decades his junior.

He has made history for so long, with such regularity, that some of us are guilty of being passive observers to that history rather than cheering with wide eyes at every remarkable turn of his career. And so it is only in recent years that Anderson has received the full measure of adulation he so clearly deserves.

The Country Music Hall of Fame and Museum's exhibit *Bill Anderson: As Far As I Can See* does justice to an incredible journey in music. Here is Anderson's story, from his sports-obsessed childhood, to his prodigious talents as a newspaper writer (he could well have forged a career in journalism), to a life as a performer and songwriter that has now lasted more than 60 years.

Bill Anderson wrote his first chart-topping hit, the Ray Price-recorded "City Lights," in 1957. Fifty years later,

Anderson won CMA and ACM Song of the Year trophies for co-writing the George Strait hit "Give It Away." In 2020 came the COVID pandemic, which found Anderson writing songs on Zoom with Brad Paisley. And when conditions allowed for a return to performing in front of audiences, Anderson was front and center on the Grand Ole Opry stage, where he has starred since 1961.

Athletes who demonstrate admirable longevity—say, Lou Gehrig or Cal Ripken, Jr.—are ultimately felled by age or illness, yet Anderson has proved impervious to such predators. His only career downturns have come when he humbly doubted the acuity of his gifts.

Anderson is a model of perseverance, of intellectual awareness, and of rare emotional intelligence. But you don't need me to tell you all of this: you can read these pages, or visit the museum's East Gallery, where we have devoted our spaces to exploring a life that will continue to be honored but will never be replicated.

Sincerely,

Kyle Young

Kyle Young | CEO

Anderson and his band, the Po' Boys, appeared in the 1965 Hollywood film *Forty Acre Feud*. FROM LEFT: Weldon Myrick, Bill Anderson, and Jimmy Gateley

5

ACKNOWLEDGMENTS

We hope this book and the exhibition it accompanies, *Bill Anderson: As Far as I Can See*, conveys the importance of Anderson's work to the story of country music writ large, and the unparalleled significance of his contribution to the art of songwriting. The book and exhibition are collaborations between Anderson, his representatives, his friends and associates, and the Country Music Hall of Fame and Museum.

We are grateful to Anderson, and to those who have loaned artifacts, documents, instruments, stagewear, and photographs, which have brought his Hall of Fame career to life and aided the book and exhibition, including Anderson, Jeannie Seely, Dean Dillon, Grand Ole Opry Archives, Hargrett Library at the University of Georgia, and WJJC Radio in Commerce, Georgia.

Also, we would like to thank Lee Willard of Straight 8 Entertainment, Scott Adkins and Kelli Wasilauski of Adkins Publicity, Judy Price, and Stephanie Orr for their contributions in making the exhibition and book possible.

Many museum staff members devoted time and talent to the book and the exhibit. Space prohibits listing them all, but some deserve mention here. Vice President of Museum Services Brenda Colladay and Executive Director of Exhibits John Reed led the curatorial team, which consisted of Peter Cooper, Mick Buck, Kathleen Boyle, Ryan Dooley, Shepherd Alligood, Kathleen Campbell, Alan Stoker, Jack Clutter, Rosemary Zlokas, and Senior Registrar Elek Horvath. Editor Paul Kingsbury, Vice President of Creative Services Warren Denney, the directors of the creative team Bret Pelizzari, Jeff Stamper, Luke Wiget, and managers Sam Farahmand and Debbie Sanders deserve special recognition.

Anderson used these headphones when he worked as a disc jockey at Commerce, Georgia, radio station WJJC in 1957.
Courtesy of WJJC Radio

OPPOSITE PAGE: Anderson and his Po' Boys mingle with fans, late 1960s

A MAN For All Seasons

BY JEANNIE SEELY

There's no expiration date on emotion. Life and love and losing . . . those things were happening when Bill Anderson started out as a writer and singer, more than sixty years ago. And those things are still happening today. Bill understands that, and he can write about his life and about our lives from every angle. He can also collaborate with other writers of all sorts, no matter the age. He never stops amazing me.

Bill hears every single thing in conversation or in a writers' room, and he dissects it immediately. Willie Nelson knows our souls. Bill gets your mind.

I met him when I first came to the Grand Ole Opry, in 1966. He was already a five-year veteran of the Opry then. I'd never even attended the Opry until I was on it, because I grew up

Anderson, c. 1970

9

in Pennsylvania and then moved to California. All of a sudden, I was shoulder to shoulder with all of these country music heroes.

Bill was so friendly and complimentary to me, immediately. He'd ask me what I thought about things, and he always valued my opinion. People aren't always so kind, and he remains that way, to everyone. At some point in our career, we're not just blessed to be at the Opry, but it's also our responsibility to make sure that the new people coming in understand what the Opry is, and what it means. It's that family membership that I most worry about disappearing, but Bill makes sure that it still exists.

I've admired the prestige Bill brought to our industry, without being flamboyant. He always brought so much class, but he's also funny and quick-witted. I asked him once, "How can the same person—how could you—write something as beautiful as 'Still' and then write something like 'Peel Me a Nanner'?" He just said, "Seely, it was a very long tour."

In some ways, that tour continues still, at the Country Music Hall of Fame and Museum.

Anderson used this custom-built Grammer guitar, with pearlescent gold finish, custom fretboard inlays, and mother-of-pearl accents on the headstock, when performing his song "Golden Guitar."

Bill Anderson and Jeannie Seely backstage at the Grand Ole Opry, c. 2001

Bill Anderson

AS FAR AS I CAN SEE

BY PETER COOPER

Bill Anderson was nineteen years old, sitting atop the three-story Hotel Andrew Jackson—the tallest building in Commerce, Georgia—when he began composing a song, imagining "a bright array of city lights as far as I can see." Commerce was a town, not a city, and the lights there consisted of a couple of stop signals. Yet Anderson pictured a "great white way" shining through the night.

Upon hearing the song Anderson wrote that steamy August evening in 1957, his father told him that he had the imagination required of a real writer. A year later, Ray Price took "City Lights" to the top of the country charts, launching a career that elevated Anderson to the Country Music Hall of Fame and earned him distinction as a Songwriters Hall of Fame member and the recipient of more than fifty BMI songwriter awards.

Anderson is a songwriter and artist of vision, and for more than sixty years he has given life to his visions with poetry and melody, while starring on the Grand Ole Opry, gaining numerous country hits as an artist, and writing monumental songs recorded by Kenny Chesney, the Louvin Brothers, Connie Smith, George Strait, and other luminaries.

This is his story.

Anderson, 1975
Photo: Raeanne Rubenstein

THE POWER
of Song

Bill Anderson was born November 1, 1937, in Columbia, South Carolina, to Lib and Jim Anderson. He was fascinated by music from the age of three and spent hours upon hours listening to Byron Parker & His Hillbillies play country music on Columbia station WIS. In late 1945, when Anderson was eight, the family moved to Georgia, settling near Atlanta, in Decatur.

Anderson learned the guitar and wrote his first song the year he turned eleven. As a high schooler, he worked part-time at his father's insurance agency, located downstairs from radio station WGLS, and he spent plenty of time watching country singers play there. His father had visions of his son following him into the insurance business, but the boy's mind was on music, writing, and sports.

Bill Anderson and his mother, Elizabeth "Lib" Anderson

His family did understand the power of song, though. His maternal grandfather was a Methodist minister. On his deathbed in 1965, at age eighty-eight, the Reverend Horace Stratton Smith told his grandson, by then a Grand Ole Opry member, "You're in a position to touch more lives with one song, with one appearance somewhere, than I've been able to touch with every sermon I've ever preached in my whole life."

Anderson used this Rawlings leather glove when he pitched for Avondale High School's baseball team, c. 1955.

LEFT: Ten-year-old Anderson at bat

OPPOSITE PAGE: The first records Anderson recalls hearing as a child were played on "Old Edison," his grandfather James William Anderson Sr.'s Edison Diamond Disc Phonograph Model C-150.

Anderson, 1942

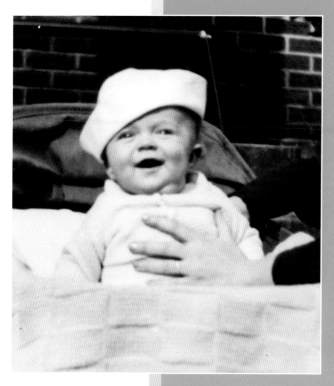

Anderson as a baby

TEENAGE *Dreams*

In the tenth grade, Bill Anderson formed a band called the Avondale Playboys and won a school talent show, on the strength of his original song "What Good Would It Do to Pretend?" The Playboys later landed a Saturday afternoon spot on WBGE, a 250-watt Atlanta radio station.

But at the time, Anderson was as interested in writing and sports as he was in music. He was a baseball pitcher at Avondale High, making up for a lack of velocity (one newspaper report referred to "the cautious left arm of Bill 'Hillbilly' Anderson") with a good curveball that drew attention from professional scouts.

This rubber Donald Duck toy—named Josh Waddlesforth McDuck—was Anderson's popular on-air sidekick at WJJC. Anderson would squeeze the toy, then interpret for his radio audience what it was saying. *Courtesy of WJJC Radio*

OPPOSITE PAGE: Anderson spinning records at WGAU, Athens, Georgia, 1956

The DeKalb New Era

C. MURPHEY CANDLER
EDITOR

W. HUGH McWHORTER
MANAGING EDITOR

PUBLISHED WEEKLY SINCE 1888
NEW ERA PUBLISHING COMPANY, INC.

Printers   *Publishers*

128 ATLANTA AVENUE
DECATUR, GA.

March 10, 1955.

Mr. Bill Anderson,
164 Conway Road,
Decatur, Ga.

Dear Bill:

I want to tell you in writing--as I have verbally--that we feel you have done an outstanding job as sports editor of the De Kalb New Era during the last two years, and are sorry to lose you.

Your stories were always accurate, interesting and well-written. If you choose sports writing as a career, I'm sure you will make a success of it.

Best of luck to you in your college career! If I can ever be of service, please let me know.

With best wishes, I am

Sincerely yours,

Joseph H. Baird

Joseph H. Baird,
News Editor.

In high school, Anderson was sports editor of Decatur, Georgia's *DeKalb New Era* newspaper, and he covered high school football and basketball games as a "stringer" for the *Atlanta Constitution*.

6 ● THE DeKALB NEW ERA ● Thursday, September 9, 1954

Sports Shots
By BILL ANDERSON

WHEN IT CAME time to pen a prevue piece on the 1954 football outlook for the Decatur high school Bulldogs, I smilingly recalled a similar article published in the New Era 12 months ago and authored by Bill Hibbert. The bold headline told the "sad" story in its entirety — **"Bulldogs At Lowest Ebb in Ten Years—Jones"** —meaning, of course, that coach Frank Jones saw only a season of gloom and defeat in store for Decatur faithful—starting with Murphy, the 1952 State AA Champs, on Sept. 11 and running through the Savannah encounter on Nov. 13.

His squad was minus such stars as Stan Thornton, Jerry Sturm, Henry Ivey, and Lucian Tatum. Why, this team would be lucky to even stay on the field!!

Of course, now this is an old story—the story of how the Bulldogs surprised everybody, ran up an 8-0-2 won-lost-tied record and only missed becoming the North Georgia AA title-holders by one point, a 6-7 loss to Grady of Atlanta . . . how Fullback John Knox made a lot of people forget Thornton, Billy Bob, the last of the Redfords, shone as Ivey never did, Tatum was replaced by All-Stater Dan Louge, and Sturm's brilliance was eclipsed by two first string quarterbacks, Earl Fuller and Charlie Maynard.

But now, they're ALL gone! In fact, 28 of Decatur's 33 lettermen of last season won't return to the grid wars this fall and Jones is moaning again.

* * *

"We've got our work cut out for us all right," says last year's Coach of the Year in region 4AA. "The squad will be largely comprised of last season's B-teamers, who, for the first time in history, failed to win a game all year. Our starters have only limited experience and we will have few reserves of proven caliber—and it's probably going to show up on our won-lost chart."

Only two of the Bulldog's five returning letter-winners were listed as starters in '53—halfback Jere Landers and guard Walter Fountain. Both are rated high by Jones and will be counted upon heavily to bolster Decatur stock. The other returnees are end Jerry Abbott, fullback Jimmy Nichols and halfback Red Howell.

It would please Jones no end to find another ball player or two the way he "found" Howell last year. It was against Gainesville that the flame-haired halfback lifted himself from B-team obscurity and led the Bulldogs to a 13-0 win, as he set up one TD and scored the other. Such a sleeper

OPPOSITE PAGE:
The Avondale Playboys, 1953

FRONT ROW, FROM LEFT: Jerry Jones, Bill Anderson, and Charles Wynn

BACK ROW: Billy Moore and Jim "Meatball" Bell

Bill "Hillbilly" Anderson, pitching for Avondale High School, c. 1955

He also wrote stories about sports for Decatur's *DeKalb New Era* newspaper, whose editor assured him he could have a successful career in journalism. Anderson had promised his parents he would go to college, and in the fall of 1955 he entered the University of Georgia to study journalism. His studies scuttled his baseball plans, but they didn't prevent him from working as a disc jockey at WGAU in Athens and eventually at WJJC in Commerce. He preferred WJJC because they let him play country music, while the WGAU brass preferred he spin rock & roll records.

The Glow
OF CITY LIGHTS

On August 27, 1957, Bill Anderson's tiny room at the Hotel Andrew Jackson in Commerce, Georgia, was stifling. As was his habit, Anderson grabbed his guitar and walked to the roof of the three-story building to catch a breeze and to look out over the small town. On a WJJC radio station envelope, he wrote lyrics that imagined a gleaming metropolis: "A bright array of city lights, as far as I can see / The great white way shines through the night for lonely guys like me."

He felt the song had promise, so he made a simple solo recording of it, which made its way to the ears of Nashville journalist and promoter Charlie Lamb, who took the record to RCA Victor producer Chet Atkins.

Atkins produced a recording of the song by RCA singer Dave Rich, and Ernest Tubb and Ray Price happened to be listening when "City Lights" was played on Nashville's WENO radio. Tubb convinced Price to record the song. Released on Columbia Records in the summer of 1958, it became Bill Anderson's first hit as a writer, a #1 country record. "City Lights" stayed on the country charts for more than half a year. Just like that, Bill Anderson—still a University of Georgia student and part-time disc jockey—was officially in the music business.

TOP: TNT Music published sheet music for "City Lights" following Ray Price's chart-topping recording of the song in 1958.

Postcard of Hotel Andrew Jackson in Commerce, Georgia, where Anderson wrote "City Lights"

OPPOSITE PAGE: Anderson, late 1950s

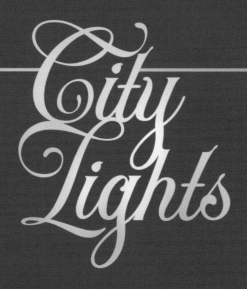

City Lights

❧ 1957 ❧

WRITTEN BY BILL ANDERSON

RECORDINGS INCLUDE: BILL ANDERSON (1958), RAY PRICE (1958), IVORY JOE HUNTER (1958),

JERRY LEE LEWIS (1965), AND WILLIE NELSON (2016)

I was nineteen years old. I was working as a disc jockey on a little radio station in Commerce, Georgia, and I was living in the tallest building in town, which was a three-story hotel. I used to like to take my guitar up on the roof of this little hotel and just sit up there and sing to the night. No audience, nobody watching me or listening to me, but it was just something I enjoyed doing. Went up there one night and looked up at the stars and the sky, and at what few lights there were in Commerce, Georgia, and ended up writing a song that changed my life called "City Lights." My father told me not long after I wrote it, he said, "Son, I should have known that you had the imagination to be a songwriter, if you could look at [the] few lights there were in Commerce, Georgia, and write about a great white way of city lights."

—BILL ANDERSON

BEHIND THE SONG

Texas-based independent label TNT Records released Anderson's recording of "City Lights" in 1958.

FROM *a Whisper to a Dream*

Bill Anderson's success with "City Lights" led to a publishing contract with Tree Publishing Company in Nashville, and soon Anderson was auditioning with producer Owen Bradley for a slot on Decca Records. With only his guitar for accompaniment, Anderson sat in the Tree office and played songs for Bradley, who said, "Well, son, you're not the greatest singer I've ever heard, but you sure do write some terrific songs. And your voice is different."

Indeed, Anderson's breathy, hushed singing style inspired comedian Don Bowman to

Decca Records publicity photo of Anderson, early 1960s

OPPOSITE PAGE, TOP: Anderson and guitarist Tommy Tomlinson on stage at KWKH-Shreveport's *Louisiana Hayride*, 1960

Early in his career, Anderson used this Royal electric typewriter to type song lyrics and answer fan mail.

dub him "Whisperin' Bill." At first the singer bridled at the nickname, but he soon realized it was a blessing. "You can look in any phone book anywhere, and you can find a William Anderson or a Bill Anderson just about anywhere that you look," he told *Billboard*. "But I'm the only one they call 'Whispering Bill,' so it's worked real good for me." It's a nickname that has stuck ever since.

In August 1958, one year after he wrote "City Lights," Anderson recorded for Bradley at the producer's famed Quonset Hut studio on Music Row for the first time, with accompaniment from master musicians including Hank Garland on guitar and Bob Moore on bass. The record, "That's What It's Like to Be Lonesome," was climbing country charts in 1959 when Ray Price heard it and recorded his own version. Price's version reached the Top Ten on the country charts, and Anderson had again proven himself as a songwriter. In early March, Anderson played hooky from his studies at the University of Georgia and went on a three-week, multi-act tour with George Morgan and Roger Miller. Late that summer, he graduated college, and soon he was living in Nashville, committed to a career as a recording artist and songwriter.

Bright Lights & COUNTRY MUSIC

On July 11, 1961, Bill Anderson was sitting in his suburban Nashville home, watching the Major League Baseball All-Star game, perhaps wondering what might have happened had he followed his hardball dreams, when his phone rang. Flustered at the distraction, he waited a few seconds to pick up the call that would change his life.

The caller was Grand Ole Opry manager Ott Devine, and he asked if Anderson would like to become a member of the Opry cast. Anderson suddenly lost interest in the ballgame and quickly accepted. "I hung up the phone and screamed loud enough to be heard in downtown Atlanta," said the man known as "Whisperin' Bill."

In the early 1960s, Anderson purchased stage costumes—including this suit embellished with rhinestones, piping, and embroidered snowflakes—by mail-order from S. A. Formann, a Western-wear tailor based in Buffalo, New York. *Courtesy of Hargrett Library, University of Georgia*

OPPOSITE PAGE: Anderson backstage at the Grand Ole Opry, c. 1961

By that summer of 1961, Anderson had already written major hits for future Country Music Hall of Fame members Roger Miller (the co-written "When Two Worlds Collide"), Jim Reeves, and Faron Young. And he was beginning to have success as a recording artist, scoring Top Ten country hits with songs he wrote, including "The Tip of My Fingers," "Walk Out Backwards," and "Po' Folks."

Anderson acquired this 1958 Martin D-28 in 1959, and for years it served as what he called his "second voice." He used the guitar extensively on stage, in the studio, and to write songs, including "Still," "The Tip of My Fingers," "Po' Folks," and "Once a Day."

TOP: Anderson at home, early 1960s

FOR IMMEDIATE RELEASE

FROM: TRUDY STAMPER
        WSM PUBLIC RELATIONS DEPT.
        NASHVILLE, TENNESSEE

JULY 12, 1961

Ott Devine, Manager of WSM's Grand Ole Opry, announced today (July 12) that
Decca recording star, BILL ANDERSON, had joined the cast of the Grand Ole Opry.
Bill will become the 48th Country Music Artist to attain STAR STATUS on the Grand
Ole Opry ... America's most famous country music program. Bill will make his first
appearance as a Grand Ole Opry star this Saturday (July 15) on the 8:00 to 8:30 P. M.
and 11:30 to 12:00 M. portion of the four and a half hour show.

Still in his early twenties, Bill Anderson is already recognized as one of America's
most prolific songwriters and gifted entertainers. As a writer, he has created such
hits as CITY LIGHTS ... THAT'S WHAT IT'S LIKE TO BE LONESOME,.... RIVERBOAT ...
FACE TO THE WALL ... and many more,....all recorded by such country music greats as
Ray Price, Faron Young, and Don Gibson. As a recording artist for Decca Records,
he has watched his own records climb in the nation's hit charts ... his latest
being ... PO FOLKS.

A former disk jockey (WGAU, Athens, Georgia and WJJC, Commerce, Georgia), last year
Bill was voted by the country's disk jockeys a place among the TOP 5 C & W Songwriters
in America and among the TOP 3 Most Outstanding New Artists in his field.

Born in South Carolina, reared in Georgia, Bill Anderson now calls himself a
Tennessean ... making his home in Nashville. He is married to the former Betty Rhodes;
they have a three months old daughter, Terri Lee.

Bill is under the personal management of Hubert Long.

WSM, the Grand Ole
Opry's parent station,
announced Anderson's
induction into the
show's cast in this July
1961 press release.

Walk Out Backwards

❦ 1960 ❦

WRITTEN BY BILL ANDERSON

RECORDINGS INCLUDE: BILL ANDERSON (1960), CONNIE SMITH (1967), AND SARA EVANS (1997)

I hadn't been married very long, and my wife and I were living in the little upstairs one-bedroom apartment over on the west side of Nashville, and we had a couple of bags of garbage that needed to be taken out. I looked up, and my wife had a bag of garbage in each hand and she was pushing the apartment door open, kind of with her backside to go out, to take the trash down to the ground. And, when I looked up from where I was sitting, instantly, it looked to me like she was bringing garbage in the house. And I thought, why is she bringing the garbage in the house? And then all of a sudden, I said, "Oh, you were walking out backwards. I thought you were walking in." As soon as that thought hit me, whoa. I think there's an idea for a song there about a guy that just tells his lady friend he's having some problems with, "Hey, if you're going to leave me, at least walk out backwards and I'll think you're walking in."

—BILL ANDERSON

BEHIND THE SONG

Connie Smith at Nashville's RCA Studio B, 1967. Her recording of "Walk Out Backwards" was included on her 1967 album *Connie Smith Sings Bill Anderson*.

THE RIGHT
Combination

Bill Anderson's presence on the Grand Ole Opry helped raise his national profile, and in 1962 he began recording a consistent string of hits that over the next fifteen years brought him to the forefront of country music recording artists. Anderson and producer Owen Bradley arrived at a template Anderson would use for several songs that featured the singer's hushed voice in recitations. The first of those was Anderson's semi-autobiographical composition "Mama Sang a Song," inspired by his mother singing in church. It was Anderson's first *Billboard* chart-topper, holding the #1 position on the *Billboard* Hot Country Singles chart for seven weeks.

The follow-up, "Still," repeated the previous record's success on country charts, and also crossed into the Top Ten of *Billboard*'s pop chart. Other versions were recorded by Bing Crosby, Al Martino, and funk legend James Brown.

Bill Anderson and Owen Bradley working in the studio, early 1960s

Anderson surveying his BMI (Broadcast Music, Inc.) awards, early 1960s

"Still" and his other recording and songwriting successes led to numerous awards, all handed out on his twenty-sixth birthday, November 1, 1963, at Nashville Municipal Auditorium, during the annual Country Music Disc Jockey Convention's awards breakfast. Leaving the awards show, singer Faron Young shouted, "Is that all you could win? I thought for sure you'd figure out a way to win Female Vocalist of the Year."

Decca promoted its latest releases by Bill Anderson and Patsy Cline with this 1963 trade magazine ad.

RIGHT: Embellished with rhinestones and embroidered quill pens and musical notes, this songwriting-themed suit was designed for Anderson by S. A. Formann in the early 1960s.

Tips of My Fingers

❧ 1960 ❧

WRITTEN BY BILL ANDERSON

RECORDINGS INCLUDE: BILL ANDERSON (1960), ROY CLARK (1963), EDDY ARNOLD (1966),
DEAN MARTIN (1970), JEAN SHEPARD (1975), AND STEVE WARINER (1992)

It's been recorded probably more than any other Bill Anderson song worldwide because it's been recorded in many different languages. It's been recorded by people like Dean Martin and Lawrence Welk and the Lennon Sisters, people totally outside of country music.

When Steve Wariner cut "Tips of My Fingers," he didn't know it at the time, and neither did I, but he was changing my life. I had written it in 1960, one of the early songs of my career in Nashville. I hadn't been living there that long. It had been a hit by myself and Roy Clark, and Jean Shepard and Eddy Arnold. I never thought it would be recorded again, but it was recorded in 1992 by Steve [Wariner] and it went all the way to #1. And I had gone through a period of time—several years—thinking, "Well, golly, maybe I've said everything that I've got to say. Maybe I've written all of the songs I'm supposed to write." I kind of lost interest in it a little bit, but when that song hit and went to #1, one day, it dawned on me, "Hey, look, you wrote that song in 1960. And it's speaking to people in 1992. You're not washed up. You just need to go back and do some more of what you were doing all these years."

—BILL ANDERSON

BEHIND THE SONG

Backstage at the CMA Awards, 1976. FROM LEFT: George Jones, Roy Clark, and Bill Anderson
Photo: Raeanne Rubenstein

❧ 1962 ❧

WRITTEN BY BILL ANDERSON
RECORDINGS INCLUDE: BILL ANDERSON (1963), BING CROSBY (1965),
BRENDA LEE (1975), AND JAMES BROWN (1979)

I remember writing "Still" very vividly. I had been on the road and I'd come home. On my road trip, I had the occasion to run into an old girlfriend down in Georgia that I hadn't seen in years. She was married. I was married. I didn't write the song for her, but I came home from that trip, and I was thinking about her and thinking about the feelings of one person seeing another person they had a relationship with—but were no longer involved with—and just the emotions of it all. And I couldn't go to sleep. I got up about three o'clock in the morning and went in my little den and wrote "Still."

—BILL ANDERSON

BEHIND THE SONG

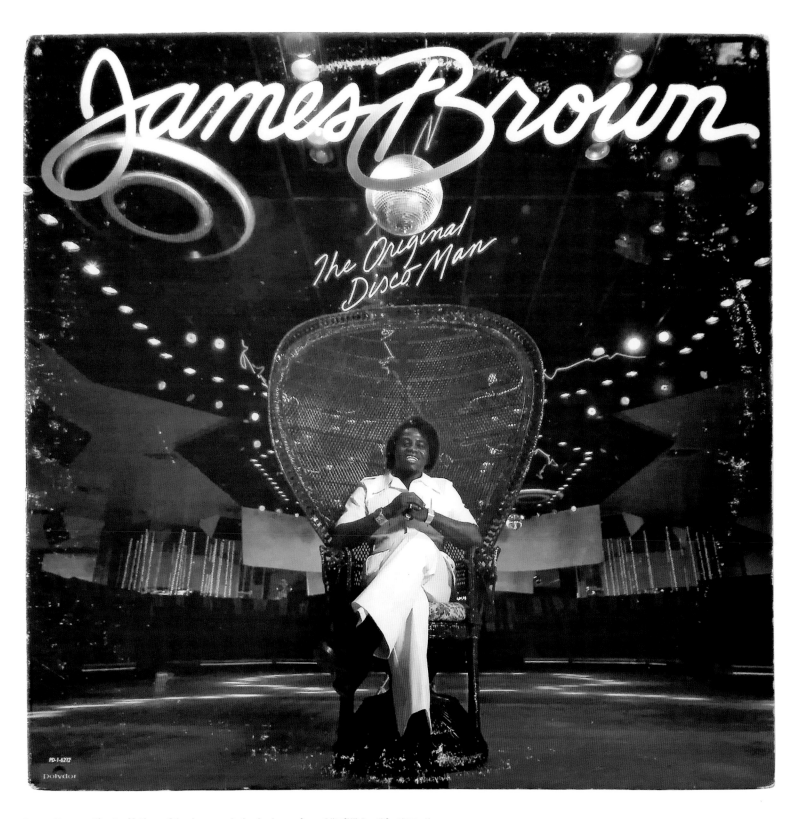

James Brown—the Godfather of Soul—recorded a funk version of "Still" for this 1979 album.

LEND A
Helping Hand

In August 1963, riding the crossover success of "Still," Anderson visited Frontier Ranch, a country music park near Columbus, Ohio, to perform and afterwards judge a talent contest. The winner of the contest—by a country mile—was a young singer named Connie Smith. Anderson told her that she had the talent to make it in Nashville if she chose to do so.

The next year, Anderson brought her to RCA's Nashville chief Chet Atkins, who signed her to the label and assigned her to producer Bob Ferguson. She entered RCA's recording studio on Hawkins Street (later known as RCA Studio B) and recorded Anderson's "Once a Day," which stayed at the #1 position on *Billboard*'s Hot Country Singles chart for eight weeks. It was the rocket launch for a career that landed Smith in the Country Music Hall of Fame. She would go on to record several songs written by Anderson and would join him as an Opry cast member in 1965.

TOP LEFT: Connie Smith wore this Malcolm Starr evening dress, adorned with beads and sequins, in the 1960s.

This reference disc contains the four recordings Connie Smith made at her first RCA session, produced by Bob Ferguson at RCA Studio B, July 16, 1964. It includes "Once a Day" and two more Anderson-penned songs.

OPPOSITE PAGE: Connie Smith signing an RCA recording contract at Nashville's RCA Studio B, while Bob Ferguson and Bill Anderson look on, 1964

At the beginning of 1965, Anderson also began hosting the syndicated TV program *The Bill Anderson Show*, a widely aired country music showcase. Among the invited guest artists was Charley Pride, who had just begun his recording career and was unfamiliar to most fans in 1966. He was also a Black man attempting to forge a music career in the segregated South. Anderson was told by the TV show's head producer that he could not feature Pride, but Anderson took a stand, and Pride's appearance on the show was a statement about country's depth and breadth.

FROM TOP LEFT:
Don Bowman and Bill Anderson on the set of *The Bill Anderson Show*, late 1960s

Anderson, c. 1965

Anderson, late 1960s

Jan Howard and Bill Anderson, late 1960s

OPPOSITE PAGE: Jimmy Gateley and Bill Anderson, 1970

I've Enjoyed
AS MUCH
OF THIS AS
I CAN STAND

Singer Jan Howard joined *The Bill Anderson Show* in 1966, and she and Anderson began recording successful duets together, including four Top Five country hits and four Decca albums between 1968 and 1972. Meanwhile, Anderson's ease and ready wit on camera led to more television opportunities. He began appearing on *Match Game*, *Tattletales*, *Password*, *Hollywood Squares*, and other daytime game shows, and even hosted *The Better Sex* on ABC. He also acted in soap operas.

Anderson used this Fender King acoustic model extensively on stage and in the studio in the 1960s and 1970s.
Courtesy of Hargrett Library, University of Georgia

OPPOSITE PAGE: Anderson on the set of *The Better Sex*, the ABC-TV game show he hosted, 1977-1978

Bill Anderson and Jan Howard on the set of *The Bill Anderson Show*, late 1960s

These were heady experiences for Anderson, but he realized he was becoming famous for things that had little to do with singing and songwriting, and by the late 1970s his records had stopped landing near the top of the charts. (His last Top Ten hit came in 1978 with "I Can't Wait Any Longer.") Meanwhile, in 1976, Anderson dissolved his professional relationship with producer Owen Bradley—a second father, in many ways—because Anderson felt it was time for a change. Anderson also made some poor investments in radio and restaurant endeavors.

He was at rock bottom creatively, feeling his best and most impactful work was behind him. "Inside, I felt like a relic," he said. "Yesterday's success does not obscure today's failure. What had I proven, other than that I used to be a songwriter?"

Bill Anderson and Mary Lou Turner—his duet partner for much of the 1970s—being interviewed at a radio station

RIGHT: This is one of several stage costumes, embellished with rhinestones and elaborate chain-stitch embroidery, designed for Anderson by Nudie's Rodeo Tailors in the 1960s.

Saginaw, Michigan

❦ 1963 ❦

WRITTEN BY BILL ANDERSON AND DON WAYNE

RECORDINGS INCLUDE: LEFTY FRIZZELL (1963), BILL ANDERSON (1965), BOBBY BARE (1966),

JOHN PRINE & MAC WISEMAN (2007), AND RANDY TRAVIS (2013)

Don Wayne, [a] great songwriter known for "Country Bumpkin," among other songs, came to me with the idea for "Saginaw, Michigan." He said he had the song started, but he didn't know how to finish it. And I'm thinking, "If Don Wayne can't finish this, how could Bill Anderson finish it?" But in my childhood, when I was seven or eight years old, and we were living in Columbia, South Carolina, we lived in a duplex apartment next to a couple from Saginaw, Michigan. So I took it home and fooled with it and came up with the idea of sending the old man up to Alaska, to look for the gold that the guy never found and he [the young man from Saginaw] ends up marrying his daughter. And Don, bless his heart, he cut me in as part-writer on the song. "Saginaw, Michigan" sat there until Lefty Frizzell heard it and recorded it. And I'm so thrilled that he did. It was the last #1 record of Lefty Frizzell's career, and it was an honor to have my name on that song.

—BILL ANDERSON

BEHIND THE SONG

LEFTY FRIZZELL
SAGINAW MICHIGAN

SAGINAW, MICHIGAN
STRANGER
WHAT GOOD DID YOU GET
(Out of Breaking My Heart)
THERE'S NO FOOD IN THIS HOUSE
WHEN IT RAINS THE BLUES
HELLO TO HIM (Goodbye to Me)
JAMES RIVER
I'M NOT THE MAN I'M SUPPOSED TO BE
THROUGH THE EYES OF A FOOL
I WAS COMING HOME TO YOU
DON'T LET HER SEE ME CRY
LONELY HEART

GUARANTEED HIGH FIDELITY

"Saginaw, Michigan" was the title track of this 1964 album by Lefty Frizzell.

A Turning Point

By the mid-1980s, Bill Anderson had spent more than two decades in the spotlight and had won numerous songwriting awards. He had been elected to the Nashville Songwriters Hall of Fame (1975) and the Georgia Music Hall of Fame (1985). Yet he was frustrated to the point of depression, wondering whether his run was over.

"My conversation with the country music audience began in the 1950s," he said. "It reached a pitched peak in the 1970s. And it grew awkward and forced in the 1980s." Could he still remain relevant as a songwriter?

The initials WBA—for Whisperin' Bill Anderson—highlight these custom-made boots by L.M. Easterling Custom Boot Company.

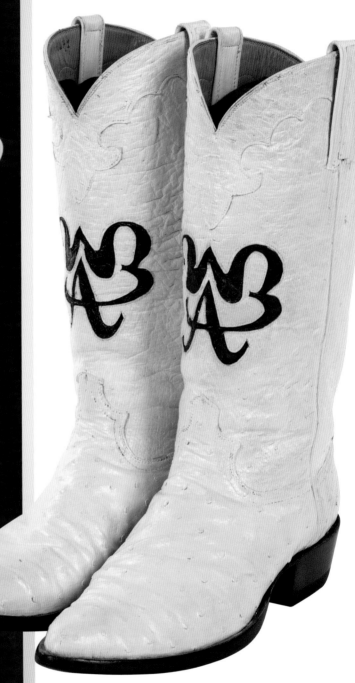

Then, in February 1992, Steve Wariner, a successful contemporary country artist, released a new single of a thirty-one-year-old Bill Anderson song, "The Tips of My Fingers," and Wariner's version sailed to #3 on *Billboard*'s country singles chart.

"Steve's version of 'Tips' was some indication that words, melodies, and emotions can carry across decades," Anderson said. With that thought in mind, Anderson opened up to the notion that he could retain relevance, years after he had doubted his place in contemporary country. He was inspired to return to songwriting.

THE NASHVILLE SONGWRITERS ASSOCIATION
HALL OF FAME
BILL ANDERSON
TWELFTH OCTOBER NINETEEN HUNDRED SEVENTY FIVE

TOP: Bill Anderson and Little Richard at the Georgia Music Awards, 1984

Anderson was elected to the Nashville Songwriters Association International (NSAI) Hall of Fame in 1975.

53

A BRIDGE
to Cross

Bill Anderson likes to say he owes his "second life" in music to a hairstylist. In the early 1990s, Cheryl Riddle was the hair stylist for both Anderson and Vince Gill, who was by then one of country music's biggest stars. Riddle encouraged Anderson to call Gill—twenty years his junior—about writing a song together. Anderson was uncertain that the young phenom would even know who he was, but the veteran swallowed his pride and phoned the number Riddle had given him.

The call went to voicemail, and the outgoing message said, "Hi, this is Whisperin' Gill. I'm not here right now." It was a very good omen. Eventually, the two men got together to write, with great success. Anderson, who had written songs by himself for most of his career, began to get comfortable with "co-writing" (that is, collaborating on ideas for lyrics and melodies until a song is created).

One of the first songs Anderson and Gill wrote together was "Which Bridge to Cross (Which Bridge to Burn)," which became a Top Five country hit in 1995. "'Bridge' knocked down a door that I'd thought was closed forever," Anderson said. Suddenly, co-writing seemed like a fine idea, and Anderson began calling other writers for appointments. "More importantly," he said, "they started calling me."

Anderson on stage, 1996

OPPOSITE PAGE: Custom built by Crafters of Tennessee, this guitar with engraved mother-of-pearl pickguard and ornate mother-of-pearl inlays on the fingerboard and headstock was a gift to Anderson from vintage-guitar collector Mac Yasuda in the early 1990s.
Photo: Elek Horvath

Cincinnati, Ohio

❧ 1963 ❧

WRITTEN BY BILL ANDERSON

RECORDINGS INCLUDE: BILL ANDERSON (1964), CONNIE SMITH (1967),

TOMMY COLLINS (1968), AND OSBORNE BROTHERS (1991)

I was between flights at the old Cincinnati Airport, and in those days you could walk around the airport, walk outside and go back in, long before we had all the security we have today. And I was standing out on the sidewalk. I just looked up at the sign that said: Cincinnati Municipal Airport. I could see the airport was kind of elevated, and I could see down towards the river—the Ohio river that flows through there. And I'm thinking one side of that river is the South and the other side spits into the North. Cincinnati, where the river winds across the Mason and the Dixon line. So it just all kind of came together, and it was a song that I didn't have my guitar or anything, but I wrote the melody. I heard the melody in my head, which I don't do very often, but sometimes I do.

—BILL ANDERSON

BEHIND THE SONG

Country and Western Music Night at Cincinnati's Riverfront Stadium, August 15, 1970. Cincinnati Reds catcher and future Baseball Hall of Fame member Johnny Bench introduces Bill Anderson, Jan Howard, and the Po' Boys prior to a game between his team and the Philadelphia Phillies.

Once a Day

∾ 1964 ∾

WRITTEN BY BILL ANDERSON

RECORDINGS INCLUDE: CONNIE SMITH (1964), CHARLIE LOUVIN (1964), BILL ANDERSON (1965),
MARTINA MCBRIDE (2005), AND VAN MORRISON (2006)

In the '60s, I was writing nearly everything by myself. I was driving my car through the suburbs of South Nashville. I have no idea where I was going or why I was there, but I remember pulling up to a four-way stop sign at the corner of Granny White Pike and Tyne Boulevard, [a] pretty upscale part of the Nashville suburbs. I don't know where that [song] came from. I had a pen and a piece of paper in the car, thank goodness. I wrote the first verse and the chorus sitting there at that four-way stop sign. I went home, got my guitar, and finished it that night. I had heard Connie Smith singing on a talent contest up in Ohio and had presented her to some record companies in Nashville. Chet Atkins said he would record her at RCA if I would write songs for her. Next thing we knew she recorded it, and the rest is history. It became a #1 record right out of the box for an artist who was doing her first recording. It's amazing.

—BILL ANDERSON

BEHIND THE SONG

Backed by Bill Anderson's Po' Boys, Connie Smith performs at Nashville's Centennial Park, August 9, 1964.

Three A.M.

❧ 1964 ❧

WRITTEN BY BILL ANDERSON AND JERRY TODD

RECORDED BY BILL ANDERSON (1964)

A fan of mine named Jerry Todd, in Cleveland, Ohio, sent me the song, and she just had the number 3 and the letter "A" and the letter "M." And that just—that kind of hit me between the eyes. I thought what an unusual title and idea. Although she had written it about a woman whose husband had left, and the woman who was up walking the floor with the baby at three o'clock in the morning. I didn't think that was the way to write the song. So I just wrote it about a guy who was walking the streets at three o'clock in the morning, wondering where his significant other was at the time. And it ends up in the last verse that the guy is going to go jump in the river and kill himself. I think the part that Bob Dylan liked was the part about, "In the news they'll say he couldn't even swim. And he gave his life for love at 3:00 a.m." I've never talked to Bob Dylan about it, but I'd like to, and I'd like to fuss at Joan Baez for not letting him finish singing [it] in that movie they made.

—BILL ANDERSON

BEHIND THE SONG

Bill Anderson and steel guitarist Sonny Garrish at Columbia Studio B, late 1960s

THE *Thrill* OF *Creation*

By the mid-1990s, for the first time in a couple of decades, Bill Anderson felt creatively on fire. He wrote often with Steve Wariner, and their co-written "Two Teardrops" became a #2 country hit for Wariner in 1999. That same year, "Wish You Were Here" (written with Skip Ewing and Debbie Moore) became the first #1 *Billboard* country single for Anderson's fellow Georgian Mark Wills.

"I was being cheered in Nashville as one of country music's top contemporary writers in town, twelve years after I'd become eligible to join the AARP," Anderson said with some amusement at the turn his life had taken. He found common ground with younger writers by ignoring the years and the current or past accolades and focusing on the task at hand.

Manuel designed this shirt, embellished with rhinestones and metallic embroidery, for Anderson in the 1990s.

Steve Wariner and Bill Anderson at the Grand Ole Opry, December 20, 1997
Photo: Donnie Beauchamp/Courtesy of Grand Ole Opry Archives

TWO TEARDROPS

Two teardrops were floatin' down the river
One teardrop said to the other
I'm from the soft, blue eyes of a woman in love...
I'm a tear of joy she couldn't carry
She was so happy — she just got married
I was on her cheek when she wiped me away with her glove...
I could tell from the look on her face she didn't need me
So I drifted on down and caught me a ride to the sea.

The other tear said we've got a connection
I'm a tear of sorrow born of rejection
I'm from the sad, brown eyes of her old flame...
She told him they would be lifelong companions
Left him with questions and not any answers
I was on his cheek as he stood there calling her name
I could tell he had a lot of my friends for company
So I drifted on down and caught me this ride to the sea.

Chorus;

Oh the ocean's a little bit bigger tonight
Two more teardrops somebody cried
One of them happy — one of them bluer than blue..
The tide goes out — the tide comes in
Someday they'll be teardrops again
Doing the things that tears are born to do
Released in a moment of pleasure or a moment of pain
Then they drift on down and ride to the sea again.

This Manuel jacket, embellished with rhinestones and embroidery, was designed for Anderson, c. 2000.

"A blank sheet of paper is a blank sheet of paper, whether you've written one hundred hit songs or never written one," Anderson said. "It's the great equalizer, and it's intimidating. But if you can transform that blank sheet into words and melody, rhythm, and rhyme, that's a victory. That's the thrill of creation, and that edge of the knife never dulls."

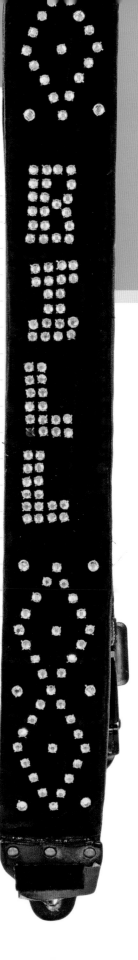

Steve Wariner
② 1-20-99

3rd V.

Two Teardrops (re-write)

Last night I sat in the waiting room
The nurse walked in and gave me the news
You've got a baby girl + they're both fine —
An old man sitting not two feet away
Just lost his wife — and he said to me
(Stm) "You've got a brand new angel + I've lost mine —
"I Guess the Good Lord giveth + the Good Lord taketh away"
And we both wiped a teardrop from our face —

2nd Cho —

The tide goes out + the tide comes in
+ A whole new cycle of life begins
Where tears are part of the pleasure
And part of the pain —
Till they drift on down and ride to the sea again.

These two sets of lyrics illustrate the songwriting evolution of "Two Teardrops."

OPPOSITE PAGE: Anderson composed the first two verses and chorus, which he typed before showing the song to Steve Wariner.

TOP: Anderson and Wariner collaborated on lyrics to a third verse and additional chorus, handwritten by Anderson.

RIGHT: Anderson has used this rhinestone-studded guitar strap extensively since the 1970s.

Award Winning

SONGS IN THE 2000s

In April 2000, Bill Anderson sat in a writers' room at Sony/ATV Publishing with singer-songwriter Jon Randall Stewart. They wrote a song that seemed at odds with contemporary radio trends, which tended towards happy, up-tempo numbers. Anderson and Stewart's song was a ballad about alcoholism and suicide: "He put that bottle to his head, and pulled the trigger / And finally drank away her memory" was the beginning to the chorus of "Whiskey Lullaby," a song that was recorded by Brad Paisley and Alison Krauss in 2003, sold two million copies, and won the 2005 Country Music Association Song of the Year award.

"Give It Away" was named Song of the Year, 2007, by both the Academy of Country Music and the Country Music Association.

In 2006, "Give It Away," a #1 hit for George Strait that Anderson wrote with Jamey Johnson and Buddy Cannon, won Song of the Year designations from both the CMA and the Academy of Country Music. At this point, in the 2000s, Anderson was also writing songs recorded by Paisley, Kenny Chesney, Joe Nichols, Sugarland, and many others. "My late-life reality has been far richer than any ought-to-be I could have imagined," said Anderson, now in his eighties and still doing exactly the same thing he was doing in August 1957 when he set pencil to paper, lyric to melody, and wrote "City Lights."

FROM LEFT: Brad Paisley, Bill Anderson, Buck Owens, and George Jones accept the award for Vocal Event of the Year for "Too Country" at the CMA Awards, 2001. Paisley's recording of "Too Country" featured guest vocals from Country Music Hall of Fame members Anderson, Jones, and Owens.
Photo: Alan Mayor

Whiskey Lullaby

❧ 2000 ❧

WRITTEN BY BILL ANDERSON AND JON RANDALL

RECORDINGS INCLUDE: BRAD PAISLEY, FEATURING ALISON KRAUSS (2003),

JON RANDALL (2005), AND BILL ANDERSON (2020)

Jon Randall and I had a writing session scheduled, and I tried to go to a writing session with some kind of an idea of something. I had the idea to write a song called "Midnight Cigarette." He picked up his guitar, and his first thing he sang was "put the bottle to his head and pulled the trigger." I said, "Forget about 'Midnight Cigarette'—we're going to write about putting the bottle to somebody's head and pulling the trigger." We ended up using "midnight cigarette" as the opening line.

People weren't running down Music Row in those days saying, "Please write me a double-suicide drinking song," but it got to Brad Paisley. And Brad is the one that took it and had the conception, the idea, to turn it into a duet. And I said, "Whoa, I hadn't even thought about that. Who are you thinking of?" He said, "There's only two people that could do it: Alison Krauss or Dolly Parton." I said, "I love them both. Go ahead." Next thing I knew, he had worked it out and did it with Alison Krauss, and it was pure magic.

—BILL ANDERSON

BEHIND THE SONG

4-12-00
Jon Randall
⑤

"Whiskey Lullaby"

She put him out
Like the burning end of a midnite cigarette
She broke his heart —
And he spent his whole life tryin to forget
We watched him drink his pain away — a little at a time
But he never could get drunk enough — to get her off his mind
Until the night —

Cho.

He put that bottle to his head and pulled the trigger
And finally blew away her memory
Life is short but this time it was bigger
Than the strength he had to get up off his knees —
We found him with his face down in his pillow
With a note that said "I'll love her till I die"
And when we buried him beneath the willow
The angels sang a whiskey lullabye —

Some times at night   For years & years
She can almost feel him in the dark   She tried to hide
She hurts so bad   the whisky on her
                                        breath
                    killed herself

The rumors flew — But nobody knew how much she blamed
                                                    herself
For years & years
She tried to hide the whisky on her breath
She finally drank her pain away — etc.
But she never could get drunk enough —

A Lot of Things Different

❦ 2001 ❦

WRITTEN BY BILL ANDERSON AND DEAN DILLON

RECORDINGS INCLUDE: BILL ANDERSON (2001) AND KENNY CHESNEY (2002)

Dean Dillon is one of the greatest songwriters that Nashville has ever seen, and he's a member of the Songwriters Hall of Fame, the Country Music Hall of Fame. He called me the night before we were going to get together, and he said, "Let's meet for breakfast. Let's get a little better acquainted before we try to write a song together." So we met in Nashville, over near Music Row, about 7:30 the next morning, had breakfast, and he told me a little bit about his life, and I told him a little bit about my life. We really left there, I think, with an understanding of kind of who each other was, and where we were each coming from. We got over to his office, and we just started reminiscing about his life and my life, taking a lot of what we had talked about at breakfast and putting it into the song [about] that point in your life, you look back and you say, "If I could do it all over again, I'd do a lot of things different."

—BILL ANDERSON

───── **BEHIND THE SONG** ─────

Dean Dillon at Mountain High Music Festival, Crested Butte, Colorado, 2018
Photo: Robert Clark/Courtesy of Dean Dillon

Give it Away

∽ **2006** ∽

WRITTEN BY BILL ANDERSON, BUDDY CANNON, AND JAMEY JOHNSON
RECORDINGS INCLUDE: GEORGE STRAIT (2006) AND BILL ANDERSON (2007)

I got into co-writing in the mid-'90s, found out it was something I really enjoyed. I loved writing with Buddy Cannon—great record producer and good songwriter. And Jamey Johnson, who's about as different from Bill Anderson, musically, as you could imagine. We were together one morning—I didn't really come with any preconceived notions, and neither did Buddy, and Jamey looked up and picked up his guitar and said, "Well, I'm going through a divorce." I said, "Well, anybody that's going through a divorce and can't write a country song needs to turn in his guitar." So Jamey started strumming and singing about the night in Frisco Bay.

—BILL ANDERSON

—————— **BEHIND THE SONG** ——————

Jamey Johnson joins Bill Anderson on stage at Nashville's Ryman Auditorium for duets on "Give It Away" and "Everybody Wants to Be Twenty-One," July 17, 2019.
Photo: Terry Wyatt/Getty Images

IT'S ALL
In The Game

Bill Anderson's love of music is rivaled but not eclipsed by his love of sports. He's a super-fan of Tennessee Titans and Georgia Bulldogs football, but his chief sporting love is baseball. An excellent pitcher in high school, he received flirtations from the Chicago Cubs before choosing songwriting and school over hypothetical glory. But he retains a deep interest in America's pastime and has befriended numerous Atlanta Braves players, coaches, and staff members through the years. Upon attending Braves spring training games, he signs as many autographs as do the players. He also maintains a close relationship with the Cincinnati Reds organization, and the Reds play Connie Smith's version of the Anderson-penned "Cincinnati, Ohio" at each home game.

Major League Baseball's Sparky Anderson—who led the Cincinnati Reds to World Series championships in 1975 and 1976—presents his number 10 Reds jersey to Bill Anderson, whose song "Cincinnati, Ohio" is a home-crowd favorite at Reds games.

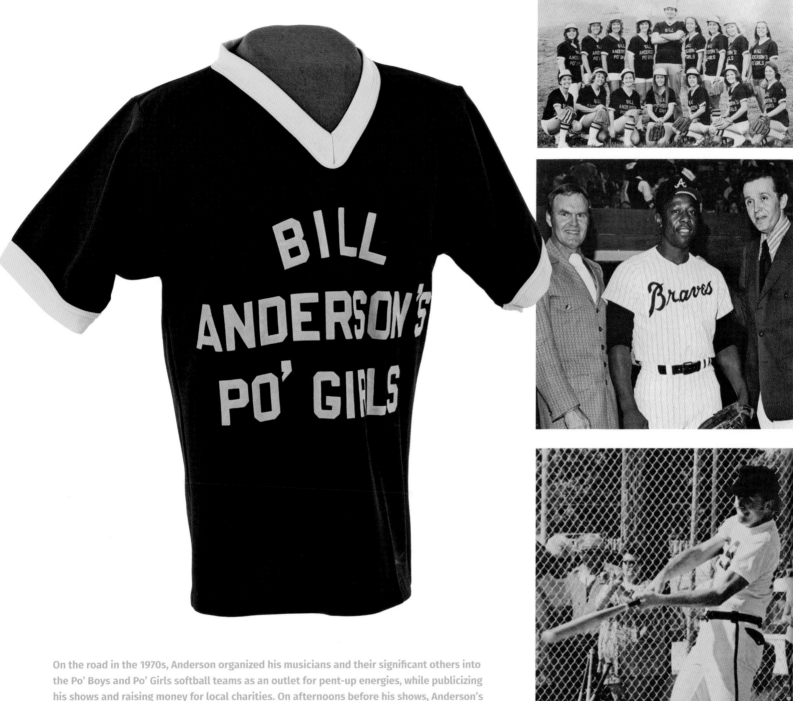

On the road in the 1970s, Anderson organized his musicians and their significant others into the Po' Boys and Po' Girls softball teams as an outlet for pent-up energies, while publicizing his shows and raising money for local charities. On afternoons before his shows, Anderson's teams—dressed in black and gold jerseys—competed against local disc jockeys and musicians.

MIDDLE RIGHT: Atlanta Braves right-fielder and future Baseball Hall of Fame member Hank Aaron meets Jimmy Gateley and Bill Anderson, c. 1970.

BOTTOM RIGHT: Anderson at bat, 1970s

BILL ANDERSON
Still

Anderson was inducted into the Songwriters Hall of Fame in 2018.

OPPOSITE PAGE: Anderson celebrates his sixtieth anniversary as a member of the Grand Ole Opry, July 17, 2021. The date was proclaimed "Bill Anderson Day" by Tennessee's Governor Bill Lee and Nashville's Mayor John Cooper. *Photo: Chris Hollo Courtesy of Grand Ole Opry Archives*

Bill Anderson remains an active force on Nashville's Music Row. Of late, he has completed several solo albums, collaborated with Country Music Hall of Fame members Bobby Bare and Dolly Parton on new album tracks, and has even written songs via Zoom with Brad Paisley during the pandemic.

Anderson recently celebrated his sixtieth anniversary as a Grand Ole Opry member, and he serves as an elder statesman and beloved ambassador for the historic radio show.

In 2001, at the beginning of what he calls his "second career" as a songwriter, he was inducted into the Country Music Hall of Fame. He has also been inducted into the all-genre National Songwriters Hall of Fame (2018) and several other halls of fame. 2021 saw Connie Smith's 1964 recording of his song "Once a Day" added to the Library of Congress's National Recording Registry, alongside works by Hank Williams, Bob Dylan, Irving Berlin, and other songwriting greats.

Anderson has placed eighty records on the *Billboard* charts as a recording artist, and his songs have been recorded by performers as varied as James Brown, Dean Martin, Willie Nelson, Charley Pride, the Louvin Brothers, Elvis Costello, Jerry Lee Lewis, Kenny Chesney, and many more. His is a rich and enduring legacy of song that extends by the day.

COUNTRY MUSIC FOUNDATION, INC.
2021 BOARD OF OFFICERS AND TRUSTEES

Mary Ann McCready, Board Chair · Steve Turner, Chairman Emeritus

E.W. "Bud" Wendell, Chairman Emeritus · Kyle Young, Chief Executive Officer

CIRCLE GUARD

The Country Music Hall of Fame and Museum Circle Guard unites and celebrates individuals who have given their time, talent, and treasure to safeguard the integrity of country music and make it accessible to a global audience through the Museum. The Circle Guard designation ranks as the grandest distinction afforded to those whose unwavering commitment to the Museum protects the legacies of the members of the Country Music Hall of Fame, and, by extension, the time-honored achievements of all who are part of the country music story.

2021 GUARD

Steve Turner, Founder

Kyle Young, Commander General

David Conrad

Bill Denny

Ken Levitan

Mary Ann McCready

Mike Milom

Seab Tuck

Jerry B. Williams

Po' Boys drummer Len "Snuffy" Miller, late 1960s